Days to your Best Life

FOR WOMEN

HONOR HB BOOKS

Inspiration and Motivation for the Season of Life

COOK COMMUNICATIONS MINISTRIES
Colorado Springs, Colorado • Paris, Ontario
KINGSWAY COMMUNICATIONS LTD
Eastbourne, England

Honor® is an imprint of
Cook Communications Ministries, Colorado Springs, CO 80918
Cook Communications, Paris, Ontario
Kingsway Communications, Eastbourne, England

40 DAYS TO YOUR BEST LIFE FOR WOMEN
© 2006 by Honor Books

Manuscript written by Susan Sealy
Interior photo © Peter Chen
Cover Design: BMB Design

First Printing, 2006
Printed in the United States of America

2 3 4 5 6 7 8 9 10 Printing/Year 11 10 09 08 07 06

Unless otherwise noted, all Scripture quotations are taken from the New American Standard Bible®, Copyright © 1960, 1962, 1963, 1968, 1971, 1972, 1973, 1975, 1977, 1995 by The Lockman Foundation. Used by permission. (www.Lockman.org). Scripture marked NIV is taken from the HOLY BIBLE, NEW INTERNATIONAL VERSION®. Copyright © 1973, 1978, 1984 International Bible Society. Used by permission of Zondervan. All rights reserved.; AB are taken from the Amplified® Bible, Copyright © 1954, 1958, 1962, 1964, 1965, 1987 by The Lockman Foundation. Used by permission. (www.Lockman.org); NKJV™ are taken from the New King James Version®. Copyright © 1982 by Thomas Nelson, Inc. Used by permission. All rights reserved; and Scripture quotations marked MSG are taken from *The Message*. Copyright © 1993, 1994, 1995, 1996, 2000, 2001, 2002. Used by permission of NavPress Publishing Group. Italics in Scripture have been placed by the author for emphasis.

ISBN 1-56292-705-1

Day 1: Experiencing God's Best

The people who know their God
will display strength and take action.
–Daniel 11:32

CROWDS OF PEOPLE in New York City witnessed an incredible event as they scanned the skyline on April 7, 1974. Thousands of feet up, a lone tightrope walker demonstrated perfect balance as he crossed on a wire between the two World Trade Center towers. His confidence showed as he jumped up and down in the middle of his crossing. He amazed even the police officers waiting to arrest him at either end. The crowds below were spellbound. For the tightrope walker, Philippe Petit, the event was the product of six years of preparation. He knew he was the best, and he was anxious to prove it.

Moving toward your best life is going to involve something of a balancing act also—finding that place of peace between God's strength and your response to it. As Daniel stated in the verse above, those of us in a committed relationship with God demonstrate strength and initiative. With Paul we declare, "I can do all things through Christ who strengthens me" (Phil. 4:13 NKJV). We understand from the very beginning that it is by God's strength, his very presence in our lives, that we accomplish anything. He has all the power. And yet he has chosen to invest power in us in what Paul refers to as a "mystery, which is Christ in you, the hope of glory" (Col. 1:27 NIV). Our response to Christ's presence in us becomes our spiritual journey, an exciting opportunity to follow wherever he leads.

Be encouraged that God is leading you on this journey. His desire is that you are "strengthened with power through His Spirit in the inner man, so that Christ may dwell in your hearts through faith" (Eph. 3:16–17). As you commit these forty days to the Lord, ask him to teach you new things about following his lead and walking out your part.

O LORD, *thank you for bringing me into your family through Christ's death on the cross. Thank you, Lord Jesus, for living in my heart through your Spirit. Please help me to follow you wherever you lead, and teach me how I can do all things through you as you work in me.*

Day 2: Enjoying God Forever

Not only is this so, but we also rejoice
in God through our Lord Jesus Christ,
through whom we have now received reconciliation.
—Romans 5:11 NIV

IF SOMEONE ASKED YOU what the whole purpose of being a Christian is, how would you answer? Serving him? Obeying him? Loving him? For many of us, the ultimate purpose gets blurred by the frantic pace of our days, by the pressures, stresses, and agendas that drive them. And sometimes the frustration of seeing our own failures and inconsistencies causes us to lose sight of God's original purpose for our lives. You might feel that it takes all your effort just to tread water and keep your head above water. God can become just one more person in your life pressing you for something you don't have the energy to give. When you're experiencing these seasons in your life, it's good to remind yourself of something taught by early church fathers and echoed by others over the centuries: Man's chief end is to glorify God and enjoy him forever.

Glorifying God and enjoying him go hand in hand. As you're enjoying God, he is glorified. Imagine having adult children who enjoyed being with you more than anyone else. Wouldn't you be honored? Wouldn't you in some ways feel "glorified"? So does God. The word *enjoy* means to experience with pleasure or to relish. He created you to enjoy him as he does you. When you relish being loved by him, he's glorified. He's not looking for some performance-oriented, I'm-going-to-do-this-if-it-kills-me relationship. He just wants to love and be loved. He just wants you.

As you go through this day, try not to focus on your spiritual anxieties but, instead, rejoice in God's presence in your life. Yes, there are a lot of truth-based principles that can bring greater freedom and benefits to your life as you pursue them. But even in that pursuit, take time to breathe deeply and remember that it's all about enjoying God and basking in his love.

HEAVENLY FATHER, *thank you for being in my life. Help me to experience you to the fullest, without anxiety and guilt. Teach me what it means to enjoy you forever.*

Day 3: Leaning on Him

We have heard of your faith in Christ Jesus
[the leaning of your entire human personality on Him,
in absolute trust and confidence in His power, wisdom,
and goodness] and of the love which you [have and show]
for all the saints (God's consecrated ones).
—Colossians 1:4 AB

DO YOU REMEMBER STARTING out on trips with your family years ago and almost immediately expressing frustration that it was taking so long? Remember asking, "Are we there yet?" We've all experienced impatience while waiting for certain outcomes.

Oftentimes we apply that same attitude to our spiritual lives. As you live from day to day, it's important to remember that your spiritual journey is just that—a journey. It takes time to make it down the road. You may have growth spurts that propel you forward, but you'll also have times when old thoughts and patterns of behavior reassert themselves.

You might disappoint yourself, wondering why you're so inconsistent. At those times in particular, it's important to lean on the Lord. Just take a step, even a baby step, in the direction you think the Lord would have you go. Offer him whatever you can in the way of attitude or action—no matter how small—and expect to see him do great things with it in your life.

Hebrews 10:14 (NIV) says, "By one sacrifice he [Jesus] has made perfect forever those who are being made holy." When you became a Christian, you were made perfect in God's eyes. That was a one-time event. In your day-to-day experience God is teaching you how to live that, how to follow the leading and teaching of the Holy Spirit inside you. It is a process. You're not going to be 100 percent consistent, but God will be faithful to make the best out of your mistakes as you lean on him.

Do you feel ready to give up in some areas? Please don't. Ask God to show you even the smallest steps of obedience you can take to lean on his direction as you pray:

LORD JESUS, *please help me not to be overwhelmed but to trust you. Show me how I can learn to trust your leading in a way that will get me past the hurdles that block me. Thank you for always being there for me.*

Day 4: Encountering God's Love

In this is love: not that we loved God,
but that He loved us and sent His son
to be the propitiation for our sins.
—1 John 4:10

IT'S WONDERFUL TO BE loved. When we're in a really good love relationship we feel a little less vulnerable, a little less alone in handling the stuff that might ordinarily pull us down. Love increases our enjoyment of each day and our hope for the future. Love gives us an edge, a little more freedom to go after what we want. It provides a place of safety from which we can enter other relationships or situations with more confidence.

Wouldn't it be great to be in that kind of life-changing

love relationship every day? As Christians, that is the reality. God's love is the starting point of our entire experience in Christ. He deeply loves us and cares about even the smallest details of our lives. He doesn't give love like you might give encouragement to someone. He *is* love. It's not a part of who he is; it's his identity. He loved us before we responded to Christ, but now through Christ he's free to enjoy us and partner with us in this journey called life.

His desire for us is that we live life out of the overflow of his love inside us. That doesn't mean that everything is going to go perfectly every day, but it does mean we're not alone. We can view our experiences from a fuller perspective—one that includes God and his purposes for our lives. We can remember that he's already paid a huge price to be in this love relationship with us and now, with Christ in us, we're part of him. Not loving us would mean not loving himself. Nothing can change that.

Seek to encounter God's love today in a tangible way. Remember specific times he's demonstrated his love for you. Now begin to thank him as you speak this prayer:

HEAVENLY FATHER, *thank you for your all-encompassing love for me. Thank you for the many different ways you've demonstrated your love in my life. Help me to walk in that love today and to respond with total love and trust from my heart.*

Day 5: Experiencing God's Grace

Therefore let us draw near with confidence
to the throne of grace, so that we may receive mercy
and find grace to help in time of need.
—Hebrews 4:16

MOST OF US BEGAN dreaming about having children early in our lives. For some of us it began as early as three or four when we held our first baby dolls. God began dreaming about his children, looking forward to your birth— onto this earth and then into his family—since long before he formed you in your mother's womb. You're not a random creation, but rather a planned child God could love and enjoy through relationship. He has always been ready to shield you with his own life because he wanted to enjoy you forever and shower you with his blessings. He just wanted to flat out love you. That unmerited favor towards you is his grace.

It's God's richness in grace that meets us when we fail and restores us. His grace envelops us as sinners and pulls us to him through the shed blood of Christ. We call it salvation. God continues giving us grace as we move forward in Christ, overshadowing our failures with his forgiveness and helping us walk through repentance each time we fall short. There's also the sense of grace that involves empowerment—not just the gift of God but God himself, the gift. God's very presence lives within us and helps us to be what he wants us to be. By grace his presence in us begins to prevail. We renew our minds with his Word, we demonstrate his character through the fruit of the Spirit, and we bring God's message to a dying world. That's the transforming power of grace.

No matter where you are on your spiritual journey, God's grace is there for you. He encourages you in 2 Peter 3:18 (AB) to "grow in grace." As you seek his best in your life, ask him to teach you how to do that—how to experience his favor and empowerment to the fullest in your life.

O GOD, *I am so grateful for your grace, which accepts me and also changes me. I want to grow in that grace—in my experience and my understanding of it. Will you please teach me more about following Christ by your grace?*

Day 6: Enjoying God's Forgiveness

Of Him all the prophets bear witness
that through His name everyone who believes
in Him receives forgiveness of sins.
—Acts 10:43

FORGIVENESS. WHAT A GREAT gift to give! Forgiveness means you're no longer holding something against someone but granting them full pardon. You're offering someone freedom—freedom from guilt, freedom from obligation, freedom from the past. You're also giving him or her a chance to start over with a clean slate. Think about how that same new beginning applies to you as a Christian. Ephesians 1:7 (NIV) says, "In him we have redemption through his blood, the forgiveness of sins, in accordance with the riches of God's grace." Notice the present tense of that verse. God's forgiveness is the gift that keeps on giving. Every day the blood of Christ covers our sin, and we can walk in authentic freedom. We don't need to question our worth. We don't need to prove ourselves. We can't do anything to pay the penalty. God wants you to feel just as free and excited as you would be if the bank called and forgave every debt you owe.

Sometimes women find it difficult to experience the benefits of freedom. Though we may believe it's available, for one reason or another we don't feel it's for us. We can become like the woman who lived and died in poverty with a million dollars stashed under her mattress. We can choose to be women who have total forgiveness but who don't accept it, never feeling release from the past. But God doesn't want that for us. The bottom line is that he wants us to hang out with him, to look forward to walking and talking with him. He's taken away any awkwardness so we can experience his presence to the fullest.

Which attitude prevails in your life: guilt or joy? Are there events and situations in your life in which you need to accept forgiveness once and for all? Ask God to take you to a new level of freedom as you pray:

O GOD, *I want to walk in the total forgiveness you've provided through Jesus Christ's death on the cross for me. I lay my past at the foot of the cross right now in exchange for your forgiveness. Help me to let go of the guilt I often feel and enjoy the freedom and joy you have for me.*

Day 7: Resting in God's Peace

Let the peace of Christ rule in your hearts,
to which indeed you were called
in one body; and be thankful.
—Colossians 3:15

IF YOU'VE LIVED NEAR a lake, you know that the most peaceful time of day is early in the morning. The wind has died down and the water is almost perfectly still. The surface lacks the turbulence caused by boats and skiers crisscrossing the water. Even when the wakes and wind cause choppy waters, all remains calm deep underwater. Unruffled by all the activity on the surface, life underneath will go on undisturbed. That's the same kind of peace that God makes available to us in Jesus Christ. It's a fruit of his

Holy Spirit released within us, not based on what we're going through but based on the nature of God.

When anxious thoughts disrupt that peace, you're encouraged to "be anxious for nothing, but in everything by prayer and supplication with thanksgiving let your requests be made known to God. And the peace of God, which surpasses all comprehension, will guard your hearts and your minds in Christ Jesus" (Phil. 4:6–7). In essence, God is saying, "Talk to me. Let me know what's going on inside you. Be honest, and let your honesty be accompanied by thankfulness as you remember all the times and ways I've been there for you." No matter how chaotic and choppy the circumstances of your life, God helps you find peace on the inside. Thanking him as you pray is one of the first steps in releasing supernatural peace in your heart. Being thankful redirects your thoughts to the rock of Jesus Christ, a rock that's unmovable and unchanging and well able to carry you through the storm.

Which concerns and anxieties make it difficult for you to enjoy God's peace on a regular basis? Consider unloading those cares onto God as you pray:

DEAR LORD JESUS, *thank you for being my rock. Help me to let go of the burdens I try to carry by myself. I know you died to carry those burdens for me. I give them to you now and ask for your peace that passes understanding to fill my heart and mind. Thank you for caring for me.*

Day 8: Letting Go of the Past

I do not regard myself as having laid hold of it yet;
but one thing I do: forgetting what lies behind
and reaching forward to what lies ahead,
I press on toward the goal for the prize
of the upward call of God in Christ Jesus.
—*Philippians 3:13–14*

IT'S HARD TO MAKE it to age twenty-five without some kind of baggage from our past—hurtful words, damaged relationships, missed opportunities, maybe a broken dream or two. Sometimes bad things have happened to us that weren't our fault; in other cases we were at fault. Either way, we often carry all this stuff as if it defines us. God wants to take that whole load off our backs. He invites us to leave it all at the cross. Even though we may have some situations we need to rectify, God wants us to let go of the past and cultivate an attitude of looking forward.

Of course, that's not always easy to do. Women often have more emotions invested in the past than our male counterparts do. Nevertheless, it's important for us to break those ties that bind us to past relationships and situations that were not of God. As we put them under the blood of the cross once and for all, we'll find new freedom to be excited about our future walk with the Lord. Looking forward to what God has in store brings an excitement and energy into the present.

It's like the week before you go on vacation. Knowing something worth celebrating is just ahead makes it easier to handle someone being rude to you today. As we cultivate that forward-looking perspective, we'll be able to walk more easily in our identity in Christ. We may still have issues to deal with in our spiritual journey, but we're looking ahead to health and wholeness and not back at brokenness and defeat.

Take a moment to think about burdens you've carried for a while that you need to relinquish. Christ is willing and able to carry your burdens. Hand them over to the Lord and begin to anticipate release in your life as you speak this prayer:

LORD JESUS, *thank you for dying on the cross for me. Help me break off any ties my soul has with past people and situations that led me away from you. Teach me how to press forward toward all you have for me as your disciple.*

Day 9: Overcoming Guilt and Failure

And we know that God causes all things
to work together for good to those who love God,
to those who are called according to His purpose.
—Romans 8:28

FAILURE IS SUCH a negative word. We all hate to fail, but we all do. There have been times in the past when we've all blown it—words we've spoken, ways we've lived, choices we've made. Because there is no way to change those actions, feelings of guilt attached to these failures often become oppressive. But God doesn't want us weighted down by any sense of failure or guilt. Through the shed blood of Christ, he's dealt with our failures once and for all. His desire is that we accept his forgiveness and redemption, for "if anyone is in Christ, he is a new creation; the old has gone, the new has come!" (2 Cor. 5:17 NIV).

Think about this: Science only moves forward as it discovers the error in its current body of truth. In other words, we can only advance our understanding of medicine and accomplish something like a heart transplant now because we've learned from our previous mistakes. In the same way, God uses our failures to teach us and mature us. To be sure, it would be great if we never made poor choices. But isn't it wonderful that God redeems the mistakes in our lives to take us to a deeper level of understanding and truth? Maturity is not an event—it's a process continuously supported by his grace and unchanging love. As we confess our failures and lay them down on the altar, we can experience the peace of God's forgiveness and enable him to redeem our actions for his glory.

Yesterday you broke any ties you had with the past. Today, take it a step further and dump the guilt. You can expect God's best for your life when you surrender all your guilt to him. Exchange it for true freedom in Jesus Christ as you pray:

O HEAVENLY FATHER, *thank you for taking care of my guilt on the cross through Christ's death. I surrender all the guilt I carry around to you, and I don't want it back. Help me to walk in the true freedom that's mine in Christ Jesus.*

Day 10: Letting Go of Bitterness

See to it that no one comes short of the grace of God;
that no root of bitterness springing up causes trouble,
and by it many be defiled.
—Hebrews 12:15

ROOTS ARE ESSENTIAL TO the growth of plant life. They anchor the plants in the soil and deliver essential minerals and water needed for growth. When a fire wipes out a forest, the nutrients stored in the root systems are vital for reforestation. In other words, the welfare of the plant above the ground is determined by the health of its root system below the ground. The significance of the role roots play reminds us of how much our behavior is influenced by what is not seen. As this verse in Hebrews indicates, negative thoughts and feelings that we have allowed to root inside us may end up doing great damage to us, as well as to those around us.

None of us wants to be bitter. We don't want to be damaged, and we certainly don't want to hurt others. But sometimes without realizing it we've allowed emotional wounds to fester and become unseen roots of bitterness. That bitterness pops up when we're in situations that connect us to the original pain. Enjoying God's best in our lives involves being willing to take inventory and let God bring healing to those wounded areas through the power of forgiveness—our forgiveness of those who have hurt us. As we are willing to acknowledge and forgive those people, we'll begin to see bitterness replaced with joy.

Are there people you need to forgive? Jesus emphasized how important our forgiveness of others was several times: when he taught the disciples how to pray, when he was teaching about communion, and when he was dying on the cross. Ask him for the grace to forgive those people who have hurt you the most.

O LORD JESUS, *I ask you to forgive me for carrying grudges in my heart. I don't want to have any roots of bitterness in my life. Please give me the grace to forgive those people you've reminded me of. I look forward to your love replacing the hurt and anger I've felt in the past.*

Day II: Valuing Yourself

Love your neighbor as yourself.
—*Leviticus 19:18* NIV

WHAT IMBUES SOMETHING WITH value? Does an item become less valuable when someone labels it as worthless? Is something still valuable even if the person who possesses it doesn't acknowledge its value? Suppose you have a $100 bill. You think it's worth something, but someone else says it's just a piece of green paper. Which view is correct? Actually, both are. The $100 bill is just a piece of green paper, but it's uncommon paper. This piece of green paper can be used to purchase $100 worth of goods or services. Why is that? Because this 2 1/2" x 6" piece of green paper is backed by the authority of the government, which has set its value at $100. You can crumple it up, throw it on the floor, and say it's nothing, but it still has a value of $100.

You may struggle at times with your sense of self-worth. Determining your value on the basis of how you feel or how others view you is a human-centered value system based on a sliding scale. Your value isn't based on who you are or what you do, but on who Jesus is and his evaluation. Real freedom from your own feelings and evaluations will come when you embrace God's unchanging value system and see yourself through his eyes. Yes, you are just a single human being, but you are an uncommon being because God has declared you to be his child and established your worth by sacrificing the life of his beloved son.

How great is God's love toward you! Take time to thank him for being willing to give so much for your salvation. You mean the world to him. Ask him to give you a true sense of your self-worth as you pray:

DEAR GOD IN HEAVEN, *thank you for valuing me so highly that you were willing to allow your son to die in order that I might live and know you. Help me to see myself from your perspective and to gain new understanding of who I am in you.*

Day 12: Flowing with Change

But we all, with unveiled face,
beholding as in a mirror the glory of the Lord,
are being transformed into the same image
from glory to glory, just as from the Lord, the Spirit.
–2 Corinthians 3:18

GOING THROUGH CHANGE is not easy. That's why one pastor who wanted to move the grand piano in his church from one side of the stage to the other, moved it four inches a week until it was across the stage. Oftentimes, we feel more comfortable with our old ways—as unsatisfying as they might be—than we do with the new. We see this clearly demonstrated as the people of Israel kept asking to go back to the slavery of Egypt rather than to trust God with their unknown future. Second Corinthians 5:17 says that when we became Christians, "old things passed away; behold, new things have come." As unsettling as that might be, God longs to see transformation in many areas of our lives—habits, desires, activities, thoughts, and even our friends.

It takes faith to follow where God is leading, but faith opens the door for his greatest blessings in your life. God intends to complete a work in you—it's part of the faithfulness of who he is—and that will probably involve taking you out of your comfort zones and into new situations. But you can trust him in the process. Think of the butterfly trying to work her way out of the cocoon. If someone breaks open the cocoon for her, she'll fall to the ground and die. It's the transforming process of biting through and wiggling free from the cocoon that builds her wings and readies her to soar beautifully from bush to bush.

Are you holding on to anything that God has prompted you to release? Trust him when he says he wants to transform you from glory to glory. Ask the Lord to give you the grace to change as you pray:

DEAR LORD, *I want so much to grow in you. Help me to trust you as you bring about change in my life. Help me to escape situations in my life that are not honoring to you and embrace all that you have for me in Christ Jesus.*

Day 13: Learning to Trust

Look at the birds of the air, that they do not sow,
nor reap nor gather into barns, and yet
your heavenly Father feeds them.
Are you not worth much more than they?
—Matthew 6:26

THE GREAT SINGER George Beverly Shea made famous the song, "His Eye Is on the Sparrow." In his deep baritone voice, Shea sang at Billy Graham crusades about the trust-worthiness of Jesus, his constant friend. He described how Jesus could help him get through tough emotional times—times of discouragement, loneliness, and darkness. The song ends with a similar image of the loving care of God: "His eye is on the sparrow, and I know he watches me."

What a strong image that is for us to think about. In the vastness of the universe, God is even aware of the needs of the littlest sparrow. This image brought comfort to a newly divorced woman in the process of making a transition from a salaried job to a commission-only job selling mortgages. She had been battling fears concerning her potential drop in income as she realized just how many mortgage brokers were already in the marketplace. As the fears began to overwhelm her, God brought this song to her mind. She started singing it over and over, getting louder and more confident with each repetition. The Lord assured her that just as there are always enough worms to go around for the birds, no matter how many birds, there will always be enough clients to provide a good living for her. She could rest in his care.

God cares for you in that same way. Experiencing his best for you means establishing a base of trust in your life that gives him freedom to work—bringing you into this or that relationship, moving you from one job to another, leading you from day to day. You can trust him fully with all your needs as you pray the following prayer:

O HEAVENLY FATHER, *I thank you that you care about even the smallest needs in my life. I thank you for all the ways you've met my needs in the past. Please help me to trust in you and in how you lead me in every situation in my life.*

Day 14: Knowing Who You Are

*It's in Christ that we find out who we are and what we
are living for. Long before we first heard of Christ and
got our hopes up, he had his eye on us, had designs
on us for glorious living, part of the overall purpose
he is working out in everything and everyone.*
—Ephesians 1:11–12 MSG

ROOTING OUR IDENTITY in Christ may be one of the most
important challenges of our spiritual journey. Our hearts
whisper agreement, but our egos scream to be the center of
attention. From the youngest age we learn to associate and
identify ourselves with other things—maybe a style, a brand,
a sport, or an attitude. We are praised for such things as our
looks, intelligence, athleticism, or communication skills. We

are applauded for our accomplishments. Over time, we bond our identity to these things and become known by labels such as the spelling champion, the clotheshorse, the shopping queen, or the bookworm.

Jesus Christ's desire is to help us unmask and realize our true identity, which is born out of our relationship with him. That requires real honesty. Just as Adam and Eve used fig leaves to hide their bodies, we often use appearances to hide our real thoughts and motivations and to mask our sins. All of this pretense gets in the way of truly knowing God. When Adam and Eve hid in the garden, it caused a break in their fellowship with God. When the prodigal son ran away, he left behind a father just longing to bless him. Sometimes we become so consumed with our baubles that we don't see the Lord of the universe, with his arms out-stretched, saying, "Daughter, I love you; you are mine. I long to give you rest and a far bigger purpose in this life than you can possibly imagine. Find who you are in me."

How do you define yourself? Is it by what you own? By what you do each day? Jesus Christ longs for you to find your true identity in him. Ask him to solidify his central place as Lord of your heart as you pray:

DEAR LORD JESUS, *thank you for continually teaching me what it means for you to be Lord of my life. Help me to be honest with you about any false pretenses I have in my life. Please help me to define who I am and to find all my purpose for living in you.*

Day 15: Overcoming Doubt

Immediately the boy's father cried out and said,
"I do believe; help my unbelief!"
—Mark 9:24

ALMOST ALL OF US experience doubts—doubts about God's faithfulness, his character, and even his existence. Usually we only express them to a trusted few. Or we try to ignore them and hope they are of no significance. Oftentimes in a personal crisis, when we need our faith to be strongest, we find ourselves unable to stop questioning the reality of God or the trustworthiness of his Word.

Faith comes in different degrees. Some people demonstrate bold, unshakable faith, such as the centurion who believed Jesus could heal his daughter from a distance. Jesus marveled at his great faith. But Jesus didn't seem bothered by the less solid faith of the distraught father quoted above. Jesus healed the man's son right after the father's anguished confession. Nor did Jesus seem to hold it against Thomas for doubting his resurrection; rather, he lovingly invited Thomas to touch the wounds himself. In fact, even in the moments before he commissioned his disciples to do his work throughout the world, Jesus had to look past their doubts: "But the eleven disciples proceeded to Galilee, to the mountain which Jesus had designated. When they saw Him, they worshiped Him; but some were doubtful" (Matt. 28:16–17).

Be encouraged today that Jesus works with whatever grain of faith you can muster—even if it's the size of a tiny mustard seed. It eventually grows into a huge tree that serves as a place of rest for others. That you have doubts is not the issue. What counts is that you have faith in Jesus and you trust him for growth. Jesus rejoices in that type of honest belief in all of his followers. Thank him for the faith you do have, and ask him to deepen your faith and use it to bless him and encourage others:

DEAR LORD JESUS, *thank you so much for helping me have faith to believe in you. I know it's a gift of your grace. Please forgive me for the doubts I have from time to time and continue to strengthen my faith so that I can be an encouragement to others.*

Day 16: Learning to Wait

Yet those who wait for the LORD will gain new strength;
they will mount up with wings like eagles,
they will run and not get tired,
they will walk and not become weary.
—Isaiah 40:31

HOW MUCH LONGER? It's the question we've
all asked while waiting for something special. It's the cry of
our heart when we are in the middle of a trial. It's the longing of our spirit for heaven. In our fast food, drive-through
culture, many of us find it hard to wait. It's especially hard
to wait when the environment we're waiting in is inhos-
pitable. We want change now!

Waiting takes discipline—discipline that God seems to

encourage us to learn. He asks us to trust him as we wait, while at the same time not giving in to the discouragements that surround us. Haven't we asked our children to do that? Haven't we said, "We'll see," many times? In the same way that we want our children to trust that we have their best interests in mind, God asks us to trust him. Though we long to have answers now, he asks us to believe that he will redeem the time and the frustration with something that fits with his purposes for our lives. He did that for Sarah. And also for Abraham, Joseph, Moses, and Hannah, who all waited years to receive the promises God had made them. In the midst of our waiting, he promises us we'll become stronger. Wait and grow—new energy, new strength, new maturity.

Be encouraged, and do not give in to the fear and the anxiety that whisper, "It will never happen." Let the deep-seated faith in your heart prevail over the circumstances and feelings that come at you in waves. Remember that when Peter was walking on the water towards Jesus he didn't begin to sink until he took his eyes off Jesus. In the same way, remain unaffected by circumstances by staying close to the Lord who will not disappoint you. Ask him to keep your gaze steadily fixed on him as you wait to see him work.

DEAR LORD JESUS, *thank you for keeping me from drowning in these circumstances that so often feel overwhelming. I'm trusting you with the prayers of my heart. Please give me the patience and strength to wait this out in a way that honors you.*

Day 17: Understanding Hope

Let us hold unswervingly to the hope we profess,
for he who promised is faithful.
—Hebrews 10:23 NIV

ONE OF THE MOST powerful commodities God brings into our lives is hope. Simply stated, hope is the sense we have that something good will happen. It's the expectation of positive change. When you're hopeless, you feel as though nothing will ever change. When you're hopeful, you're looking for and expecting breakthrough—something to change for the better. Over and over in the Scriptures God encourages us to hold on to hope. In fact, Romans 15:13 (NIV) refers to him as the "God of hope" and goes on to say that he wants us to "overflow with hope by the power of the Holy Spirit." No matter what you're facing today, God wants to release hope in your life. If you've gotten a bad report about your health, God wants you to know it's subject to change. If your child is going through tough times, that's subject to change. If you have oppression you can't shake, be hopeful.

Sometimes we're hit with things that seem too hard to combat even with strong faith. That's a great time to fall back into the ocean of God's hope. It's the foundation block that faith is built on. We can speak to whatever circumstances are overwhelming us and say, "This situation is subject to change. I'm holding onto hope because God always takes care of me like he's promised." As you keep expressing hope, you'll find that faith begins to grow without your even trying. Soon you'll have faith just like Abraham, "in hope against hope, he believed" (Rom. 4:18).

Today is not the day to give up. Determine in your spirit to hold onto hope no matter what and express it to God as you speak this prayer:

O FATHER IN HEAVEN, *thank you for being the God of all hope. I know that you're at work in my situation right now and that it's going to change in your timing. Please help me to hold unswervingly to that hope and to wait for deliverance from you.*

Day 18: Worshipping As a Lifestyle

Therefore I urge you, brethren, by the mercies of God,
to present your bodies a living and holy sacrifice,
acceptable to God, which is your spiritual service of worship.
—Romans 12:1

WHERE DO YOU EXPERIENCE your best times of worship? In the car? In the shower? At church? For most of us, praising and worshipping God during a church service is when our emotions most easily connect with the Lord and our devotion seems to reach its highest intensity. We might even comment to others, "The worship was really good today." But true worship isn't something that happens on the outside within a certain timeframe. As Paul indicates in this verse, true worship is a lifestyle. It begins with the surrender of our hearts to God in the midst of our ordinary days, giving him control over everything touching our lives—our emotions, our relationships, our money, our agendas, our situations.

That means that everything we do becomes part of our opportunity to live life as a worshipper—whether it's making a presentation or changing a diaper. It's not about what we're doing but about how we're doing it. God receives everything in our busy and frazzled days as worship when we've presented ourselves to him. Driving kids to school, working on a business project, responding to our husband, or singing in church are all forms of worship when they're done with a surrendered heart. And that brings God's best into our lives. It brings his peace into everything we do. We experience new mercy and grace each day. There is no more guilt because you can't accomplish everything you need to do. No anxiety about what's going to happen. It's freeing. It's calming. It's worshipping.

Enjoy yourself as you worship God today throughout all your activities. Start by presenting yourself to him right now and inviting his lordship today as you pray:

O GOD, *I thank you for being so worthy of worship. I want everything I do to honor and praise you. Let my life and everything in it be a sweet fragrance of worship to you.*

Day 19: Believing without Seeing

Jesus said to her,
"Did I not tell you that if you believed,
you would see the glory of God?"
—John 11:40 NIV

A YOUNG WOMAN WAS waiting anxiously for her boyfriend to propose. Though they'd talked about it, he hadn't yet popped the question. One weekend when she expected it to happen, he was unable to spend time with her, saying he had to study. As time went by, he seemed to spend less and less money on her. She became increasingly frustrated and impatient, complaining about his lack of attentiveness and questioning his ability to commit. What she didn't know was that he had spent the weekend in question visiting her parents and asking for her hand in marriage. Subsequently, he had invested every bit of his spare money in a beautiful diamond ring.

Those of us who knew what was going on behind the scenes saw a spiritual lesson in the situation. "If only she knew," we whispered repeatedly amongst ourselves. We wondered how often God is at work on our behalf behind the scenes while we're complaining and becoming frustrated with what we see. We thought of people in the Bible like Joseph who seemed to experience one hardship after another without comfort or explanation from God. And yet, behind the betrayal by his brothers and years spent in slavery and in prison, God was moving Joseph toward the destiny that God purposed for him. We realized how easy it was to judge God mistakenly when circumstances don't seem to be moving in our favor.

Have you judged God in some way and given up believing because he hasn't performed in the way and time you expected? His promise to us is that if we'll just believe, we'll see him glorified in the results. Thank him for the work he's doing on your behalf right now as you pray:

DEAR FATHER, *thank you that you are always at work on my behalf. Please forgive me for judging you based on what I see. Help me to wait patiently on your timing and to trust you with all my heart.*

Day 20: Cultivating Persistent Prayer

Very early in the morning, while it was still dark,
Jesus got up, left the house and went off
to a solitary place, where he prayed.
—Mark 1:35 NIV

HAVE YOU NOTICED how dependent we've become on our cell phones in recent years? It seems we can't go anywhere without them—whether we're going shopping, to a movie, or even to church. Somehow that growing dependence is connected to our need to be in communication with people. Most of us carry them just so we can enjoy conversations with others whenever we want. Conversation is one of the ways we build relationships. It's how we communicate our feelings and our needs. It's our lifeline with each other, and even more so in our relationship with our heavenly Father. Jesus demonstrated more than anyone else how prayer is a lifeline. Though his time was often monopolized by the needs of people around him, Jesus always found time to talk with his heavenly Father.

Most of us really want to deepen our relationship with God. We know that he beckons us to talk with him and bring everything to him in prayer. He encourages us with promises that our prayers make a difference. Yet we struggle with cultivating a consistent prayer life. Yes, our days are packed with myriad tasks and activities. Even so, our heavenly Father invites us into his presence now. As Hagar said when God responded to her cries in the desert, he is "the God who sees." He sees all the struggles, stress, and pressure you deal with each day. And he knows how uplifted and relieved you'll be after spending time with him. His heart calls out to you and says, "Won't you come give the load to me so that I can carry it for you?"

If you don't already have a consistent prayer life, today is a great day to begin establishing one. Ask the Lord to help you develop your relationship with him as you pray:

DEAR GOD, *thank you for continuing to teach me about prayer. I want to be more faithful in coming to you first with my needs and desires before going to everyone else. Please help me cultivate faithfulness in prayer in my life.*

Day 21: Getting Cleansed Daily

Peter said to him, "Never shall You wash my feet!"
Jesus answered him, "If I do not wash you,
you have no part with Me."

Simon Peter said to Him, "Lord, then wash
not only my feet, but also my hands and my head."
Jesus said to him, "He who has bathed needs only to
wash his feet, but is completely clean; and you are clean."
—John 13:8–10

PICTURE YOURSELF HAVING DINNER with a celebrity who brings in a bowl and kneels before you to wash your feet after dinner. Somehow the very act of that person kneeling in front of you would expose feelings that made you uncomfortable. You would probably feel strangely unworthy. You'd be embarrassed if your toenails weren't nicely manicured and your heels weren't satin smooth. That is how Peter felt—proud and humbled at the same time, embarrassed and exposed.

Jesus persisted in washing Peter's feet because he needed Peter to understand the nature of their ongoing relationship. Each day we encounter sin just like Peter did—some attaches itself to us from our surroundings and some rises up from the inside. This story illustrates our need to allow Jesus to wash the effects and influences of sin away every day. No matter how embarrassed we are or how unworthy we feel, we can humble ourselves before the Lord and let him cleanse us. Honest confession and repentance are vital to our spiritual journey. They bring us freedom from sinful attitudes, thoughts, and feelings. As we recognize them, confess them, and move in a different direction, we're able to enjoy the fullness of all that God has for us.

Let the Lord wash your heart every day. Be honest and humble before him as he reveals things to you that need to change. The freedom that you will experience as you're transformed in these areas keeps the door open for God's best in your life.

DEAR LORD JESUS, *thank you for providing the way for me to be totally forgiven of my sins. Please cleanse my heart today of anything that's not of you and make me aware of anything that needs to change.*

Day 22: Hanging Out in the Word

Do not let this Book of the Law depart from your mouth;
meditate on it day and night, so that you
may be careful to do everything written in it.
Then you will be prosperous and successful.
—Joshua 1:8 NIV

WHO'S YOUR BEST FRIEND? How did she get to be your best friend? Undoubtedly you've spent lots of time together. Probably you've gone through a lot together, sharing the exciting things that have happened as well as the harder times. You probably know what she's thinking in particular situations without even asking her—because you've developed intimacy over the years. God desires that same intimacy in his relationship with you. He wants you to know him like your best friend. He wants you to understand who he is and how he works in your life. He's revealed himself in Scripture so that you can grow to a point where you know what he thinks without even asking him. More than anything, he wants you to realize through Scripture how very much he loves you, his precious daughter.

Spending time in God's Word each day isn't a way to prove yourself to God, but it is a way to access his grace as the Holy Spirit teaches you. As you read, he gives you fresh insight and personal application. He can make his Word relevant to whatever situations you're in—better advice than your best friend can offer. God's Word is an offensive weapon to overcome even the most difficult situations.

If you're not accustomed to seeking God through his Word, try making it a regular part of your life. He would like to become more intimate with you through spending time together in the Word. Ask him to lead you in this process as you pray:

HEAVENLY FATHER, *thank you for revealing yourself through your Word. Please help me get to know you better through it. Give me a hunger to read it every day. Let your Spirit give me understanding and lead me into truth.*

Day 23: Waiting in Expectation

In the morning, O LORD, you hear my voice;
in the morning I lay my requests
before you and wait in expectation.
—Psalm 5:3 NIV

PRAYING AND WAITING—we understand that. It would be wonderful if God blessed us immediately with the answers we're looking for. Most of us realize, however, that prayer is not a snap-your-fingers experience. We're used to praying and not getting an instant response. We're used to waiting. But this statement in one of David's psalms seems to indicate that there's more to prayer than just laying our requests before God and waiting. David has something much more proactive in mind. He's referring here to an attitude that anticipates God's response and intervention. It's an attitude of expectation.

Are you expecting enough of God? Expectation can be a tricky word. Counselors would probably tell us it's important to manage our expectations. Scripture, on the other hand, encourages us to confidently believe that God hears and answers our prayers. That's what David does, despite lots of ups and downs in his life. He prays daily and then eagerly watches to see God's intervention. It may not come in the form he requested or desired at the time, but he anticipates God's response. That's praying in faith "and without faith it is impossible to please Him, for he who comes to God must believe that He is and that He is a rewarder of those who seek Him" (Heb. 11:6).

As you move forward in your prayer life, learn to pray with expectation. Believe that God wants to do more for you, in you, and through you than you can imagine. You may have been previously disappointed, but don't give up on him. He understands your vulnerabilities, which is why he treasures your faith so greatly. Ask him today to lead you in praying, waiting, and expecting:

O LORD, *thank you for hearing me when I pray. Help me to really believe in you when I pray and to anticipate your response. Teach me what it means to wait in expectation. I'm excited about seeing you work for me, in me, and through me.*

Day 24: Walking in the Holy Spirit

But the Counselor, the Holy Spirit,
whom the Father will send in my name,
will teach you all things and will remind you
of everything I have said to you.
—John 14:26 NIV

GOD IS SUCH a good father! He never intended for us to become his perfect children alone. Instead, he gave us a helper, a counselor, a guide to lead the way. This guide wouldn't be one who would just study our map and point in the direction we should go. Rather this helper from the Lord would make his home inside us and go with us on the journey. When you became a Christian, the Holy Spirit came to live inside you. As amazing as it seems, especially when you read in the Old Testament about the elaborate design and construction of Solomon's temple, your body has now become God's temple. The Holy Spirit completes your union with God, residing in you to accomplish God's will through you.

The Holy Spirit lives within us to minister to us and through us. As our teacher, comforter, and counselor, he lovingly helps us hear and respond to God's activity in our lives. He longs to accomplish what we were never intended to do in our own strength. He speaks, reveals, convicts, directs, counsels, and encourages us. He conveys God's heart to us, especially in our crisis moments. He even labors in prayer for us. He searches our hearts, knows our minds, and understands our weaknesses, and yet he works eternally to increase our intimacy with God. He ministers to those around us through the release of Christ's nature in our lives—such traits as love, kindness, and goodness. He empowers us for ministry to our neighbors, including the sick, the poor, and the captive.

As you yield to the leading of the Holy Spirit, he will fill you with his presence and continue completing that work that was started in you at the moment of your salvation. Ask him to fill you now as you pray:

DEAR LORD JESUS, *thank you for giving me the Holy Spirit to accomplish your perfect will in me. Please fill me now with his presence and help me be faithful in following his leading in my life.*

Day 25: Connecting to Community

Speaking the truth in love, we are to grow up in all aspects into Him who is the head, even Christ, from whom the whole body, being fitted and held together by what every joint supplies, according to the proper working of each individual part, causes the growth of the body for the building up of itself in love.
—Ephesians 4:15–16

IT IS SAID THAT people who are together a lot begin to act like each other. That can be an unsettling thought if you spend a lot of time with people who have unattractive traits. But for those who are Christian, connecting with others in a Christian community has the effect of maturing us together to reflect the nature and presence of Christ in the world.

The faith journey was never meant to be walked out alone. God is all about relationship. Though you were created as an individual, you were designed to complement others. This passage in Ephesians describes you as being part of the larger body of Christ. It means you'll experience greater effectiveness and maturity as you align with a community of other Christians truly seeking to honor God in their midst. You can certainly be a believer without going to church, but somehow the fullest expression of God happens when we're tightly connected to other believers. You weren't meant to journey alone. God wants us to come alongside each other through all the inevitable ups and downs of life. Others need you as much as you need them.

You may have been burned in the past by some church experience. Or you may be holding back from committing to a local church because you think you have nothing to contribute. The truth is the body of Christ is limited in its effectiveness and maturity without your involvement. Ask God to lead you in joining the community of believers as you pray:

DEAR HEAVENLY FATHER, *thank you for bringing me into the body of Christ and giving me a community to journey with. Show me where and how I should connect in order to honor you and be of the greatest use.*

Day 26: Dealing with Disappointment

If they had been thinking with [homesick] remembrance
of that country from which they were emigrants,
they would have found constant opportunity to return to it.
But the truth is that they were yearning for and aspiring
to a better and more desirable country, that is,
a heavenly [one]. For that reason God is not ashamed
to be called their God.
—Hebrews 11:15–16 AB

WE GREW UP READING stories that ended with, "and they lived happily ever after." Fairy tales. We somehow hoped our lives would have some resemblance— the happy ending, the white picket fence, even the prince. But in the world we live in now we often have a different experience that brings pain, loss, and frustration. It's the experience of disappointment.

Disappointments have a way of taking up residence in our hearts. We find it hard not to revisit them, and we find ourselves asking such questions as, "What if I'd done this" or "What if I could do it over again?" We're tempted to return to that place and rehash the past, revisit the torment, and pick at the wounds. These are our temptations to "think with homesick remembrance of that country from which we are emigrants." Yes, it's easy to go back there, but God calls us to look forward. Disappointments give us the opportunity to choose to focus on him and let him bring healing to the hurts of our past. God cherishes faith that counts on him in this way, and he takes public joy in the strength of the relationship built on faith.

Pause for a moment and think about the memories that still burden your daily existence. Do you see God as able and willing to redeem even your most grievous losses? Can you let him give you a new dream for the future? Ask him to give you the ability to look forward as you pray:

O GOD, *thank you for being the God of the brokenhearted. Thank you for sending your son to set the captive heart free. Help me to let go of the broken dreams in the past and to embrace with joy all you have for me now.*

Day 27: Developing Accountability

Make this your common practice:
Confess your sins to each other and pray
for each other so that you can live
together whole and healed.
—James 5:16 MSG

MOST OF US HAVE participated in at least one kind of weight loss program in pursuit of that well-shaped, healthy body. Probably one of the main motivations for joining is accountability. We know the pressure of having to check in with someone else will help us make it through the rough spots. When our hands reach out for dessert or junk food, we remind ourselves, "You know what? I have to weigh in tomorrow. I'm not going to eat

.this." The realization of what's ahead gives us an edge in overcoming the desire for a few bites of the dessert everyone else is enjoying right now.

The same principle applies to walking in spiritual maturity. We need others in our lives who are familiar with our faults and weaknesses—people with whom we can openly and honestly share our struggles and triumphs. Having even one relationship like this gives us a place of safety and healing when we do things we shouldn't. As James says in this verse, confessing to each other and praying helps produce health and wholeness in our lives—for several reasons. First, verbalizing our struggles or sins diminishes the tormenting power they have over us and frees us to deal with them openly. Second, we have someone to pray with, someone who knows us but doesn't judge us and can encourage us with God's wisdom. Finally, it gives us someone to help provide accountability for us in the future.

Be intentional about developing an open and honest relationship with another mature Christian. Ask the Lord to give you wisdom in finding the right person who can come alongside you in strength as you pray:

DEAR LORD, *thank you for putting other believers in my life to help me be the kind of person you want me to be. Help me to find the right person to be open and honest with, who'll speak to me from your heart and with your direction.*

Day 28: Watching Your Words

When there are many words, transgression is unavoidable,
but he who restrains his lips is wise.
—Proverbs 10:19

"STICKS AND STONES MAY break my bones, but words will never hurt me!" Has there ever been a more untrue statement? Our mothers used to teach us this when we were growing up, as if it would offer some kind of shield to hurtful words. It didn't really help. How many times have you been hurt by the careless remark or untimely criticism of another? On the other hand, how many times have you said, "I didn't mean it that way," trying to backpedal and soften something you've just said? One of our biggest challenges as women is to learn to watch our words—to make our communication whole-some, encouraging, and uplifting.

Words are building blocks in our relationships. Each day we can choose to interact with others in a way that encourages them to walk in all that God created them to be—or we can choose not to do that and risk inflicting harm. Being intentional about how we speak to people demonstrates that we value them as much as God does. He cautions us to be mindful of how powerful our words are. In fact, he goes so far as to say, "Death and life are in the power of the tongue" (Prov. 18:21). Think of how many times a word or two, spoken at just the right time, has made all the difference to you. Now think how great it would be if you consistently made that difference for other people. That doesn't mean that we can't be honest, but it does mean that we let God's wisdom, as opposed to our emotions, drive the timing, manner, and content of what we say. Ask the Lord to give you just the right words to touch someone else today as you pray:

DEAR GOD, *thank you for all the ways you encourage me through your Word. Please give me the words to encourage and build up those I come in contact with today. I want to speak your voice into the lives of those around me.*

Day 29: Choosing Not to Judge

For I am confident of this very thing,
that He who began a good work in you
will perfect it until the day of Christ Jesus.
—Philippians 1:6

REMEMBER WHEN YOUR MOTHER told you to do something a certain way and you immediately had a desire to do it in just the opposite way? There's something in most of us that reacts negatively when certain people try to tell us what to do. Fortunately, as we mature in Christ and receive God's grace, we become willing to surrender control of our lives to him. We allow him to take the driver's seat in our lives and change us from the inside out.

One of the hardest things to do when we feel God has

shown us the right way is to allow others close to us to find the path by themselves. It's hard to trust the Lord for his power and timing to work in the lives of others we love, especially our husbands and older children. Sometimes in our conviction or enthusiasm we take on the burden of changing them, which is not our responsibility. Pursuing God's best in our own lives means being at peace with how he's working in the lives of others. Trusting the Holy Spirit to guide them instead of trying to guide them ourselves frees us from feeling frustrated and judgmental. It allows us to focus on our own relationship with the Lord and move forward with the truths he desires to impart to us.

Are there any people you find yourself frequently criticizing and judging because they're not progressing spiritually as you think they should? Take a step of faith by releasing them into his care as you pray:

DEAR LORD JESUS, *thank you for loving me even with all my weaknesses and inconsistencies. Help me not to judge others who aren't living up to my expectations. Thank you that you're at work in their lives in ways I can't see and am not called to judge.*

Day 30: Staring Down Adversity

Consider it all joy, my brethren, when you encounter various
trials, knowing that the testing of your faith produces endurance.
And let endurance have its perfect result, so that you
may be perfect and complete, lacking in nothing.
—James 1:2–4

I'VE SEEN A GREETING card with a sad-looking beagle
with droopy ears accompanied by the words, "They say you
learn the most from your most difficult experiences." The
punch line on the inside says, "What a stupid system!" Those
words probably echo sentiments we've all felt at times as
we've worked through hard situations in our lives.
Sometimes the adversities we face seem too overwhelming
or too painful. And the benefit of growth and maturity

seems too insignificant or too remote. But the deeper truth this verse conveys is that there's a way to go through hard times that not only assures you of greater maturity in Christ but also empowers you in the moment.

Getting God's perspective on any ordeal you're going through helps put the problem in proportion. It reminds you that nothing is too difficult for God to handle. As you determine to let God work through your struggles, you break free of the hold they have over you. That eternal perspective allows God's peace to settle your feelings and guard your thoughts. It empowers your faith so that you can stare right into the adversity you're facing and say like David, "I will yet praise him" (Ps. 42:5 NIV). You may feel uncomfortable or insincere in displaying praise or joy in the midst of a tough situation, but God will honor even your smallest seed of faith with blessing. And the great promise here is that this experience today will produce greater strength in you tomorrow.

Are you dealing with a difficult situation right now that has stolen your joy or limited your praise? Remember that God is well able to help you come out victorious in this matter. Stir up your faith right now as you pray:

DEAR HEAVENLY FATHER, *thank you that you use everything in my life for my good. Thank you for walking me through this tough time. I trust you to use this in some way for your glory, and I thank you that you'll strengthen me though it.*

Day 31: Dressing in Power

*Lay aside the old self, which is being corrupted in accordance
with the lusts of deceit, and be renewed in the spirit of your
mind, and put on the new self, which in the likeness of God has
been created in righteousness and holiness of the truth.*
—Ephesians 4:22–24

HAVE YOU EVER POWER dressed for a specific occasion? Worn something just for the purpose of intimidating someone? Or maybe bought something new because it increased your self-confidence or made you appear thinner? Choosing what to buy and wear can make such a difference in how we feel. The clothes we wear often reflect our attitude about ourselves. The same is true spiritually. Throughout the Scriptures we're directed to clothe ourselves in ways that reflect the presence of God. In addition to putting on the new self, we're encouraged to "put on a heart of compassion, kindness, humility, gentleness, and patience" (Col. 3:12). God instructs us in his Word to put on the armor of God and love. It is important that what we wear on the outside reflect the truths we believe on the inside.

When Cinderella arrived at the ball, everyone thought she was a princess. Her beautiful gown gave her confidence and conveyed an attitude of royalty that fooled even the prince. In the same way, in Isaiah 61:3 we are encouraged to put on the garment of praise, indicating it's the antidote to heaviness and despair. Somehow, the attitude we choose to wear on the outside helps pull the truths we believe on the inside into our reality—not only lifting us, but also demonstrating Christ to those around us. Every day we have the opportunity to dress up or dress down in our spiritual attitudes. Choosing to put on the best that we have in Christ pulls his best into our experience. Ask the Lord to help you dress in his strength today as you pray:

DEAR LORD JESUS, *thank you for dwelling inside me through the Holy Spirit. Help me to clothe myself with the realities of all that you are. I want to glorify you with my attitudes every day.*

Day 32: Living in Humility

Do nothing from selfishness or empty conceit, but with humility
of mind regard one another as more important than yourselves;
do not merely look out for your own personal interests,
but also for the interests of others. Have this attitude in
yourselves which was also in Christ Jesus, who, although He
existed in the form of God, did not regard equality with God
a thing to be grasped, but emptied Himself, taking the form
of a bond-servant, and being made in the likeness of men.
Being found in appearance as a man, He humbled Himself by
becoming obedient to the point of death, even death on a cross.
–Philippians 2:3–8

LIVING IN HUMILITY BEGINS in your mind. You must
have an accurate perspective of who you are in relation to

others and to God. This passage in Philippians teaches us that Jesus Christ demonstrated humility when he died on the cross for us. Though he had the right to be treated and acknowledged as God, he obeyed God, putting himself under the control of others even though it meant his own death. He did it out of obedience, and he did it out of love.

God challenges all of us to be less self-centered and to develop more of an awareness of the needs of others on a daily basis. Our culture bombards us with messages that appeal to our vanity, ego, and ambitions. We tend to measure ourselves by the things we accumulate rather than the things we give away. But God calls us to measure ourselves in relation to Christ. He challenges us to lay down what is ours by right and to pick up the burdens of others. It's called loving your neighbor as you love yourself.

If your life was being filmed today, who would you be seen promoting—yourself or those around you? Would you be perceived as a person who grasps at power or one who uses power to serve others? Ask God to develop the same attitude in you as was in Jesus Christ as you pray:

DEAR GOD, *thank you for being patient with me even in my self-centeredness. I renounce any attitude that isn't of you and ask you to give me that same attitude as was in Christ Jesus so that I can serve those around me.*

Day 33: Developing Discipline

No soldier in active service entangles himself
in the affairs of everyday life, so that he may please
the one who enlisted him as a soldier. Also if anyone
competes as an athlete, he does not win the prize unless
he competes according to the rules. The hard-working farmer
ought to be the first to receive his share of the crops.
—2 Timothy 2:4–6

WHEN SOLDIERS ARE ENGAGED in battle, it's vital that they stay focused and work together. Lives depend on it. Each soldier needs to perform at his highest level, no matter what circumstances he has to overcome. That can only happen if he's prepared himself through extensive training. In this letter to Timothy, Paul likens a soldier to a fully-committed disciple of Christ. Still later in the chapter he refers to a disciple as a workman, a bond-servant, and a vessel. All of these images might cause us to despair if he didn't start the chapter with this affectionate encouragement: "you therefore, my son, be strong in the grace that is in Christ Jesus" (2 Tim. 2:1).

Just as it takes time for a soldier to learn to fight, it takes time for us to mature into seasoned disciples of Christ. Even as he is encouraging Timothy to develop spiritual disciplines in his life, Paul reminds him that it can only be accomplished by God's grace. "Be strong in the grace," Paul says. In other words, depend on God's strength. Discipline rises up out of that mysterious blend of your weakness and Christ's strength. In your helplessness, you're appointed to do it. Discipline accomplished through grace leads to depth and maturity. As Paul says to Timothy later in the letter, if you can find this balance you can "fulfill your ministry."

Jesus Christ says to all of us, "Follow me." Will you risk saying "yes" and follow him as far as he wants to lead you? Ask him to teach you how to draw from his grace as you pray:

DEAR LORD JESUS, *thank you for calling me to be your disciple. I want to follow you wherever you lead me. Please be my strength in developing habits of discipline and holiness that will deepen my relationship with you.*

Day 34: Walking in Favor

For it is You who blesses the righteous man, O LORD.
You surround him with favor as with a shield.
—Psalm 5:12

IT'S POSITIVELY ENJOYABLE to walk in favor with people. They appreciate you so much more, whether it's your boss, your friends, or your husband. You somehow know that they're watching your back. If you're a mother, you know what it means to show favor to your kids. Though you enjoy other children, nothing is quite the same as hugging your own. You work to secure for them the best possible opportunities and outcomes because you want the very best for them. It's all part of the love package that comes with the relationship.

God is in that same kind of relationship with you. He's the original parent. He loves showing favor to you. In fact, lots of verses indicate his delight in making good things come your way. His desire for you is that you celebrate life each day with a grateful heart that trusts him in every situation. But suppose this is a tough day. What if someone else gets the promotion you're hoping for? What if your child's teacher is mean to him or her today or a close friend hurts your feelings in some way? Does that mean his favor comes and goes? Or that you're not worthy enough to have it today?

Not at all. Know that no matter what happens today, you're in a win/win situation because your father loves you and shields you with his favor. Make an effort to recognize his favor in your daily life, believing it and thanking him for it as you pray:

DEAR HEAVENLY FATHER, *thank you so much for your favor every day and the way you shield me with it. I believe you are watching over me and causing good things to happen. I thank you for the future plans you have for me and I look forward to your blessings today.*

Day 35: Cultivating Gratefulness

Through Him then, let us continually
offer up a sacrifice of praise to God, that is,
the fruit of lips that give thanks to His name.
—Hebrews 13:15

DO YOU REMEMBER WRITING thank-you notes as a child? So many times it seemed like a forced and insincere gesture, yet it was so important to most of our mothers. They knew that the act of thanking the giver would help us realize a greater appreciation for the gift—that we would be less likely to take it for granted. And they probably also felt that the gift givers would enjoy knowing their effort was appreciated. Wise mothers seemed to know something deeper was happening in the process—the development of grateful hearts that appreciated the love and generosity of others.

Encouragement to give thanks is found throughout the Scriptures. We are encouraged to have a continual attitude of thanks and praise. We're exhorted to "enter His gates with thanksgiving and His courts with praise. Give thanks to Him, bless His name. For the LORD is good" (Ps. 100:4–5). Just like wise mothers, God admonishes us to be grateful because he knows that gratefulness not only blesses him, the giver, but also accomplishes a work in us. Our words stir up greater worship in our hearts, pulling them in the direction of our mouths. Thankfulness also helps when our hearts feel downtrodden. The "fruit of our lips" empowers our hearts, somehow overtaking negative feelings that might otherwise overwhelm us. Speaking gratefully when you're unhappy can be difficult, but we can find strength in Jesus. "Through him then" we offer a sacrifice of praise and release blessing to both God and ourselves.

Let gratefulness rise up out of your heart through your relationship with Jesus Christ. Ask him to develop a heart in you that gives thanks no matter what as you pray:

DEAR LORD JESUS, *thank you for being my strength. I want to learn to worship and praise you continually. Please develop a grateful heart in me and help me to display thankfulness no matter what I'm going through.*

Day 36: Hanging Tough

For she thought,
"If I just touch His garments, I will get well."
—Mark 5:28

THIS WOMAN HAD BEEN bleeding off and on for twelve years. It took all of her energy just to go see another doctor, let alone be out in a public place fighting the crowds. She had given up lots of times. She'd stopped going to doctors because she couldn't handle any more bad reports. She didn't have any money left anyway. But for some reason she had gained hope again—hope that God could do something, would do something, if she could just get close enough to this healer she'd heard about. She pushed her way through the crowd. Finally she made it past everyone blocking her and lunged toward him, grabbing at his cloak as she fell. Her body felt the impact immediately. She fell back, overwhelmed by the tingling heat surging through her body. A moment later Jesus turned around, searching for the one who had bumped him. She would have been afraid of his rebuke except for the overwhelming sense of peace, joy, and warmth flooding her. He studied her face, and then spoke with the most incredible confidence, "Daughter, you took a risk of faith, and now you're healed and whole. Live well, live blessed! Be healed of your plague" (Mark 5:34 MSG).

Are you, like this woman, facing a tough situation? Something that has plagued you for years? God wants you to know he hears the cries of your heart. Even if everything is closing in on you, hang tough, knowing he loves you more than words can express. Rest in his care today as you pray:

O DEAR GOD, *thank you that you've heard all my prayers and that you'll never leave me alone. Help me to continue to trust you and believe that you'll take care of me. Give me the spiritual strength to continue looking forward to your intervention on my behalf.*

Day 37: Making Your Personality Count

As each one has received a special gift,
employ it in serving one another as good stewards
of the manifold grace of God.
—1 Peter 4:10

IDENTICAL TWINS DO NOT have identical finger-prints. In fact, of all the billions of people that God has created, no two have identical fingerprints. That makes you one of a kind, uniquely designed and created by God. Your personality, with all its strengths and weaknesses, is unique. Added to your personality mix are the spiritual gifts and talents with which God has gifted you. No one else is exactly like you, and no one else can fulfill the purposes for which God has created you.

As Christians we're all part of the body of Christ. We're created as a spiritual community to complement one another in a way that demonstrates the life and character of Christ to those around us. You have something to contribute that no one else has—yourself. As you step forward and allow God to use your special mix of personality and gifts, you'll find your greatest fulfillment as a Christian. You might not step out with your significant strengths because you're afraid of looking silly or even arrogant. But trust God to lead you and help you with the counsel of others within your community. You might hang back because you think that what you have to contribute is too small or insignificant. You may have just the right word of encouragement for someone today. Or God may bring you across the path of someone who needs prayer.

You are special to God. He designed you to be just who you are. Ask him to reveal to you areas of service where he can use you specifically. Expect to see him open doors of ministry as you pray:

DEAR GOD, *I know that I am fearfully and wonderfully made and that you have uniquely gifted me to be a reflection of your love. Please give me boldness in you and enable me to reach out with your love to those around me.*

Day 38: Enjoying Your Inheritance

Doesn't that privilege of intimate conversation with God
make it plain that you are not a slave, but a child?
And if you are a child, you're also an heir,
with complete access to the inheritance.
—Galatians 4:7 MSG

CAN YOU IMAGINE how wonderful it would be to be born into a family of great wealth? Not only would you have a sense of security, but you'd also enjoy all the comforts that money could provide. Seems like life would be fairly stress free! Scripture teaches us that we have been born into just such a family—God's family. Though it may seem intangible at times, our inheritance is very real and, as the verse above implies, accessible now. We may have to wait for the streets of gold, but we can access his strength, his power, and his favor right now.

Just like loving parents, God wants to see his children enjoy the benefits that are already rightfully theirs. According to Ephesians 1:14 (AB), our down payment on the inheritance to come is the Holy Spirit. He introduces us into all-sufficiency now. He reveals to us the unchangeable, eternal God who is our Father. He brings the absolute love of God himself into our reality by grace. He conveys the power of God to our inner man. We taste and see the fruit of our inheritance now because death has already occurred—the death of Jesus Christ on the cross. Through his shed blood we're invited to begin to draw out of the spiritual realm all that's been promised to us for eternity. God has blessed us now with "every spiritual blessing in the heavenly places in Christ," (Eph. 1:3) that we "may be filled up to all the fullness of God" (Eph. 3:19).

Your inheritance in Jesus Christ is greater than the reaches of human imagination! Ask the Lord to lift the limits of your understanding that you might enjoy all that God has for you as you pray:

DEAR LORD JESUS, *thank you for sacrificing your life in order that I might know God and experience all that he has for me. Please help me to access all that is available to me now through the Holy Spirit that I might bring greater glory and honor to you as your disciple.*

Day 39: Seeking God

But seek first his kingdom and his righteousness,
and all these things will be given to you as well.
—Matthew 6:33 NIV

And without faith it is impossible to please Him,
for he who comes to God must believe that He is
and that He is a rewarder of those who seek Him.
—Hebrews 11:6

IF SOMEONE TOLD YOU there was a $1 bill hidden in your home, would you take the time to search for it? Probably not. But how quickly would you start looking if someone told you that dozens of $100 bills were hidden there? You'd probably tear your house apart. The difference is in the value of what you're seeking. You experience a burst of energy and excitement when you're searching for something of great worth to you. How much energy do you invest in seeking God? The Lord continually invites and instructs us to seek him actively.

Items that are the most difficult to obtain tend to have the most value—oil, gold, and diamonds, for example. Similarly, the Lord longs for us to search his depths. Just as you wouldn't reveal your deepest inner thoughts to a casual acquaintance, he reserves the mysteries of his nature for those who are most committed to him. Those people not only search him out but also have allowed their desire to know him to become the priority of their lives. At this level, the Lord tells us, you'll tap into the riches of all that God is and the deepest blessings he has for you. And only then will you experience full friendship and fellowship with Jesus Christ.

Seeking God takes place one day at a time. It happens as we learn to look for him in our lives—seeking him in his Word, talking with him as we go, thanking him, questioning him, loving him. God longs for a deeper relationship with you. Won't you seek him out?

O DEAR GOD, *thank you for giving me the opportunity to know you. I want to seek you and find you in the deepest possible way. Please help me to look for you every day and refuse to settle for less.*

Day 40: Enjoying Kingdom Living

For He rescued us from the domain of darkness,
and transferred us to the kingdom of His beloved son.
—Colossians 1:13

Do not be afraid, little flock, for your Father
has chosen gladly to give you the kingdom.
—Luke 12:32

THE WORLD WAS CAPTIVATED by her rescue. On April 1, 2003, fully armed American soldiers entered a hospital in Nasiriya, Iraq, and snatched Pfc. Jessica Lynch from Iraqi captivity. Wounded from her capture a week earlier when her convoy was attacked, Jessica's rescue dramatically portrayed the transfer of one person from captivity to freedom. In an equally dramatic manner, you were snatched from the kingdom of darkness and transferred to the kingdom of Jesus Christ when you became a Christian. You have become part of the body of Christ on this earth, commissioned to demonstrate his life and character to those around you by the working of his grace in you. Though the reality of your kingdom citizenship may seem elusive, it's as real as Jessica Lynch's American citizenship. And God has purpose in it for you.

God has deposited himself in you. Think about the significance of that. The Creator of heaven and earth, your Maker, somehow also dwells inside you in the person of the Holy Spirit. And he has imparted to you authority in his kingdom. As Jesus seems to imply above, that can be intimidating. But your heavenly Father planned it that way. He chose to invest his kingdom in you. Every day you have the opportunity to release what God has deposited in you. The world you've been rescued from needs what you have. You can't do it by yourself, but it can't happen without you.

Today is a great day. Rejoice in all that God has done in your life. Ask the Lord to alert you to those around you in need of his touch. Expect to see him reveal his best through you today as you pray:

PRECIOUS GOD AND FATHER, *thank you for rescuing me from the domain of darkness on this earth and transferring me into the kingdom of Christ. I invite you to complete your purpose through my life. Please help me share the good news of the kingdom to those around me.*

Additional copies of this and other Honor products
are available wherever good books are sold.

If you have enjoyed this book,
or if it has had an impact on your life,
we would like to hear from you.

Please contact us at:

HONOR BOOKS
Cook Communications Ministries, Dept. 201
4050 Lee Vance View
Colorado Springs, CO 80918

Or visit our Web site:
www.cookministries.com